SUPER
SANDCASTLE™
It's the Alphabet!

It's P!

Mary Elizabeth Salzmann

Consulting Editor, Diane Craig, M.A./Reading Specialist

ABDO
Publishing Company

D1211667

Published by ABDO Publishing Company, 8000 West 78th Street, Edina, Minnesota 55439. Copyright © 2010 by Abdo Consulting Group, Inc. International copyrights reserved in all countries. No part of this book may be reproduced in any form without written permission from the publisher. Super SandCastle™ is a trademark and logo of ABDO Publishing Company.

Printed in the United States.

 PRINTED ON RECYCLED PAPER

Editor: Katherine Hengel
Content Developer: Nancy Tuminelly
Cover and Interior Design and Production: Kelly Doudna, Mighty Media
Photo Credits: iStockphoto (Jani Bryson), Shutterstock

Library of Congress Cataloging-in-Publication Data
Salzmann, Mary Elizabeth, 1968-
  It's P! / Mary Elizabeth Salzmann.
    p. cm. -- (It's the alphabet!)
  ISBN 978-1-60453-603-4
  1. English language--Alphabet--Juvenile literature. 2. Alphabet books--Juvenile literature. I. Title.
  PE1155.S2682 2010
  421'.1--dc22
  ⟨E⟩
                    2009022026

Super SandCastle™ books are created by a team of professional educators, reading specialists, and content developers around five essential components—phonemic awareness, phonics, vocabulary, text comprehension, and fluency—to assist young readers as they develop reading skills and strategies and increase their general knowledge. All books are written, reviewed, and leveled for guided reading, early reading intervention, and Accelerated Reader® programs for use in shared, guided, and independent reading and writing activities to support a balanced approach to literacy instruction.

About SUPER SANDCASTLE™

Bigger Books for Emerging Readers
Grades K–4

Created for library, classroom, and at-home use, Super SandCastle™ books support and engage young readers as they develop and build literacy skills and will increase their general knowledge about the world around them. Super SandCastle™ books are an extension of SandCastle™, the leading preK–3 imprint for emerging and beginning readers. Super SandCastle™ features a larger trim size for more reading fun.

Let Us Know
Super SandCastle™ would like to hear your stories about reading this book. What was your favorite page? Was there something hard that you needed help with? Share the ups and downs of learning to read. We want to hear from you! Send us an e-mail.

sandcastle@abdopublishing.com

Contact us for a complete list of SandCastle™, Super SandCastle™, and other nonfiction and fiction titles from ABDO Publishing Company.

www.abdopublishing.com • 8000 West 78th Street
Edina, MN 55439 • 800-800-1312 • 952-831-1632 fax

Aa Bb Cc Dd Ee
Ff Gg Hh Ii Jj Kk
Ll Mm Nn Oo Pp
Qq Rr Ss Tt Uu Vv
Ww Xx Yy Zz

The Letter Pp

The letter **p** in
American Sign Language

P and **p**
can also look like

Pp	**Pp**
Pp	Pp
Pp	Pp

The letter p is a consonant.

It is the 16th letter of the alphabet.

Some words start with **p**.

pizza

parrot

peach

plate

Patty

Patty put pieces of pizza and peach pie on plates for her pet parrots.

Some words have **p** in the middle.

spider

newspaper

April

April was surprised when she opened the newspaper and a spider jumped out.

Some words have **p** at the end.

soup

cup

Kip

Kip got soup on his top lip when he took a sip from his cup.

11

Some words have a double **p**.

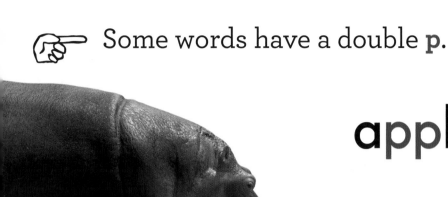

apple

hippo

The happy hippo dropped an apple by the napping puppy.

puppy

ph as in **ph**otograph

trophy

When the letter p has an h after it, it often sounds like f.

elephant

Joseph won a trophy for his photograph of an elephant talking on the phone.

phone

Perfect!

It's P!

Patrick Panda comes up with the perfect plan to keep cool.

He calls all his pals and invites them to play by the pool.

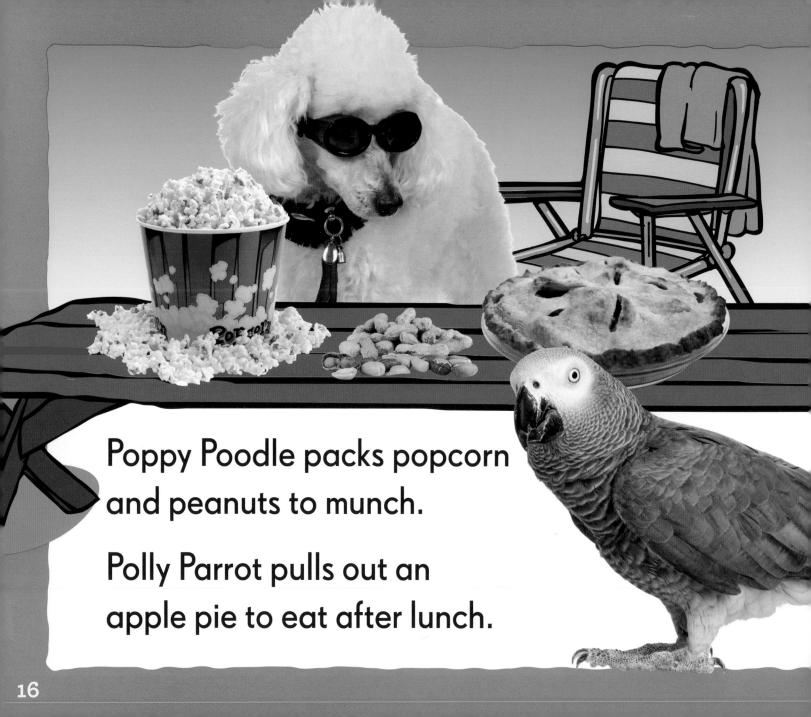

Poppy Poodle packs popcorn
and peanuts to munch.

Polly Parrot pulls out an
apple pie to eat after lunch.

Spike Spider spies spinach salad and split pea soup.

Chip Chipmunk brings enough pizza for the whole group.

Penny Penguin prefers fruits like grapefruit and pears.

She chomps on a peach while perched on a chair.

Skippy Hippo has pitchers
of punch and soda pop to sip.

He also puts out potato chips
and spicy chip dip.

Patrick and his pals hope
the party never stops.

They jump into the pool
with flips and belly flops.

Which words have
the letter **p**?

peas

cup

chipmunk

hummingbird

koala

phone

notebook

puppy

Glossary

belly (p. 20) – stomach.

chip (p. 19) – a very thin slice of potato that is cooked in oil.

chomp (p. 18) – to bite or chew something.

grapefruit (p. 18) – a large, round fruit that is yellow on the outside and pink on the inside.

munch (p. 16) – to chew or snack on.

perch (p. 18) – to sit or stand on the edge of something.

photograph (p. 13) – a picture made using a camera.

pitcher (p. 19) – a container with a handle used to hold and pour liquids.

salad (p. 17) – a mixture of raw vegetables usually served with a dressing.

split (p. 17) – to cut in half.

trophy (p. 13) – a prize given to the winner of a competition.

To promote letter recognition, letters are highlighted instead of glossary words in this series. The page numbers above indicate where the glossary words can be found.

More Words with **P**

Find the **p** in the beginning, middle, or end of each word.

beep	lap	picture	pot	sheep
cap	pan	pig	present	sleep
cop	paper	pin	price	spring
gap	pat	plant	pumpkin	tap
help	pay	please	purple	zip
hop	people	pony	rip	zipper